Table of Contents

All about Penguins

All about Penguins

Katie Peters

GRL Consultant Diane Craig,
Certified Literacy Specialist

Lerner Publications ◆ Minneapolis

Lerner Publications
An imprint of Lerner Publishing Group, Inc.
241 First Avenue North
Minneapolis, MN 55401 USA

For reading levels and more information, look up this title at www.lernerbooks.com.

Main body text set in Memphis Pro 24/39
Typeface provided by Linotype.

Photo Acknowledgments
The images in this book are used with the permission of: © Chayasit Fangem/Shutterstock Images, p. 3; © CherylRamalho/Shutterstock Images, pp. 4–5; © ChameleonsEye/Shutterstock Images, pp. 6–7; © BeautifulBlossoms/Shutterstock Images, pp. 8–9, 16 (right); © Gerald Corsi/ iStockphoto, pp. 10–11, 16 (center); © Lea McQuillan/Shutterstock Images, pp. 12–13, 16 (left); © Liz Leyden/iStockphoto, pp. 14–15.

Front cover: © Rajh.Photography/Shutterstock Images

Library of Congress Cataloging-in-Publication Data

Names: Peters, Katie, author.
Title: All about penguins / Katie Peters.
Description: Minneapolis : Lerner Publications, [2025] | Series: Let's look at polar animals (pull ahead readers - nonfiction) | Includes index. | Audience: Ages 4–7 | Audience: Grades K–1 | Summary: "There are many different kinds of penguins, but they all protect their eggs the same way. Engaging photographs and leveled text help young readers learn about these birds. Pairs with the fiction text, Pedro's Family"—Provided by publisher.
Identifiers: LCCN 2023031592 (print) | LCCN 2023031593 (ebook) | ISBN 9798765626306 (library binding) | ISBN 9798765629284 (paperback) | ISBN 9798765634523 (epub)
Subjects: LCSH: Penguins—Juvenile literature.
Classification: LCC QL696.S473 P459 2025 (print) | LCC QL696.S473 (ebook) | DDC 598.47—dc23/eng/20230713

LC record available at https://lccn.loc.gov/2023031592
LC ebook record available at https://lccn.loc.gov/2023031593

Manufactured in the United States of America
1 – CG – 7/15/24

Penguins are birds. There are many kinds of penguins.

They cannot fly. But they are good swimmers.

They swim to find food.
They eat fish.

Penguins lay one or two eggs. The parents hold them on their feet.

Soon the baby chicks hatch.

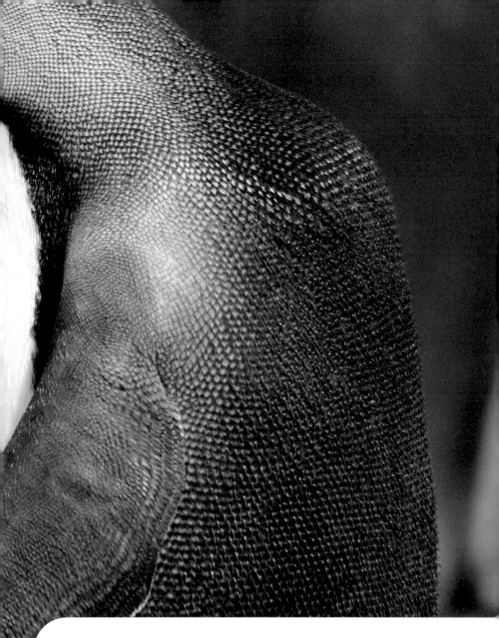

The parents feed the chicks.

Did You See It?

chick   egg   fish

Index